A QUICK GUIDE TO

Teaching Reading Through Fantasy Novels

5–8

Other Books in the Workshop Help Desk Series

A Quick Guide to
Reaching Struggling Writers, K–5
M. COLLEEN CRUZ

A Quick Guide to
Teaching Persuasive Writing, K–2
SARAH PICARD TAYLOR

A Quick Guide to
Making Your Teaching Stick, K–5
SHANNA SCHWARTZ

A Quick Guide to
Boosting English Acquisition in Choice Time, K–2
ALISON PORCELLI AND CHERYL TYLER

A Quick Guide to
Teaching Second-Grade Writers with Units of Study
LUCY CALKINS

A Quick Guide to
Reviving Disengaged Writers, 5–8
CHRISTOPHER LEHMAN

For more information about these and other titles,
visit www.firsthand.heinemann.com.

WORKSHOP HELP DESK

A QUICK GUIDE TO

Teaching Reading Through Fantasy Novels

5–8

MARY EHRENWORTH

Workshop Help Desk Series

Edited by Lucy Calkins

with the Reading and Writing Project

firsthand

HEINEMANN

DEDICATED TO TEACHERS™

HEINEMANN

Portsmouth, NH

DEDICATED TO TEACHERS™

An imprint of Heinemann
361 Hanover Street
Portsmouth, NH 03801–3912
www.heinemann.com

Offices and agents throughout the world

Library of Congress Cataloging-in-Publication Data
Ehrenworth, Mary.
 A quick guide to teaching reading through fantasy novels, 5–8 / Mary Ehrenworth.
   p. cm. — (Workshop help desk series)
 ISBN-13: 978-0-325-04281-7
 ISBN-10: 0-325-04281-0
 1. Reading comprehension—Study and teaching (Elementary). 2. Reading comprehension—Study and teaching (Middle school). 3. Children—Books and reading. 4. Fantasy fiction. I. Title.
 LB1573.7.E37 2011
 372.47'2—dc23   2011020368

SERIES EDITOR: *Lucy Calkins and the Reading and Writing Project*
EDITORS: *Kate Montgomery and Teva Blair*
PRODUCTION: *Victoria Merecki*
COVER DESIGN: *Monica Crigler and Jenny Jensen Greenleaf*
COVER PHOTOS: *John Hallett*
INTERIOR DESIGN: *Jenny Jensen Greenleaf*
COMPOSITION: *House of Equations, Inc.*
MANUFACTURING: *Veronica Bennett*

Printed in the United States of America on acid-free paper
15 14 13 12 11 VP 1 2 3 4 5

For
Jackson Ehrenworth, Torrin Hallett, and Tanner Hallett,
who taught me what powerful reading looks like,
and whose knowledge of fantasy inspired this book

CONTENTS

PART THREE: LITERARY TRADITIONS

A Note on Why to Read Fantasy, and What to Expect in this Unit

Picture this: three boys, ranging in age from fifth grade to ninth grade. Torrin is explaining why Dumbledore had to die. Tanner agrees then notes how an event in the last *Harry Potter* novel is connected to something that happened almost three thousand pages prior, in an earlier novel. Jackson begins to talk about the different symbols in the novels. Then they begin a fast-paced-interrupting-each-other-chant of their favorite fantasy series. "I *love* that one . . ."

I have observed this conversation in classrooms. But where I see it again and again, is in between kids who are avid fantasy readers. They talk to each other on trains and planes, in hallways and cafeterias. They are *expert*. In some ways, this unit of study is not about teaching avid fantasy readers how to be more powerful—they already read and talk about these books with passion and wisdom. It's more about learning with these expert readers, and bringing their insightful practices to less nuanced readers. They read with a passion and an avidity and a stamina that we would love to see in all our readers. It would be crazy for us not to tap that passion, and even crazier for us not to try to instill it in all our readers. This is bigger than our own tastes. It's about harnessing the power of literature that is productive for readers. And listen, even reluctant readers will love these books. You can't read *The Lightning Thief* and not fall in love with it. If you get to dystopian literature as part of this study, *The Hunger Games* is an unstoppable force. Get a kid or adult into that novel, and you have created a life-long reader.

There are underlying reasons that fantasy reading may be compelling for adolescents. Kieran Egan, in his study, *Romantic Understanding: The development of rationality and imagination, ages 8–15,* notes that adolescents are peculiarly powerless, and therefore, at this age they experience what he calls "an urge to transcend the conventions that surround us, to remake the world closer to our heart's desire" (1990, p. 111). Or as Laura Miller wrote in her *New Yorker* article, *Fresh Hell: What's Behind the Boom in Dystopian Literature for Young Readers,* "the world of our hovered-over teens and preteens may be safer, but it's also less conducive to adventure" (June 14, 2010). Teens yearn for adventure. And they yearn to be different than they are. It's what Michael Chabon calls in his novel, *The Amazing Adventures of Cavalier and Clay,* 'caterpillar dreams': dreams of fabulous escape and transformation. It is the urge to be transformed, to become like Harry Potter, whose ordinary life becomes extraordinary, whose private problems take on epic meaning. There is something vividly satisfying about fantasy. It fills a yearning, deep within us, the yearning to achieve significance.

If that's what fantasy does for their souls, here's what fantasy does for our students as readers: It lures them into reading epic novels that span, especially across series, hundreds to thousands of pages. These readers will develop thematic understanding, inevitably, as fantasy novels overlay their themes prominently on the storyline. They will practice the highest level of synthesis, as they put together the clues about what kind of place this is, who has power and control, what is at stake, and how the characters fit into it all. And they learn to revise their understanding, to wait and ponder, and rethink and reconceptualize. And then when they go to the next series, they are better readers. They know more. The books teach them. Everything that standards such as the Common Core Standards, and state tests and reading curricular and literature classes emphasize—synthesizing events, characters, and places, interpreting themes and moral lessons, understanding the literary tradition from which a novel emerges, is the natural fodder of fantasy reading. I know that if I can teach kids to be powerful readers of fantasy, they can learn to read pretty much anything—because they'll have learned to tackle dense, long texts with unfamiliar settings and vocabulary, they'll learn to move across complex narratives, nonfiction field guides, accompanying blogs and websites—it's an intertextual, intellectual cornucopia.

The Structure of the Unit

This unit fits within structures Lucy Calkins researched, devised, and describes in detail in *Units of Study for Teaching*

Reading (Heinemann, 2009), including time across the week for instructional read aloud, mini-lessons that teach specific reading strategies, independent reading time in class and outside of class, and partnerships. You'll find the *Units of Study* series, written by Calkins and colleagues, helpful in planning a yearlong reading curriculum. If you're a middle school teacher, you'll want to particularly turn to: *Navigating Nonfiction; Tackling Complex Texts: Historical Fiction in Book Clubs*; and the additional units for experienced readers, in *Constructing Curriculum: Alternate Units of Study*.

Here's how this unit goes. First we launch the kids into fantasy book clubs or partnerships—the kids are going to want to talk about these books, and you'll want to channel this urge to heighten their intensity and stamina for literary conversations. In the first part of the unit, we'll teach the kids to read with deep comprehension and to synthesize across pages. Then we'll move in the second part of the unit to developing their thematic understanding, and finally in the third part we'll develop their expertise of literary traditions so they begin to see the book they are holding as part of a grander, conceptual text set. Across these parts of the unit and the weeks of the unit, the students will read several books—often they will tackle at least one series, and sometimes they'll move across series. If you have enough time for read aloud almost every day, then you can read aloud *The Lightning Thief*, which anchors these lessons. But you could also read aloud shorter texts such as *Dragon Slayer Academy*, which is short, engaging, and remarkably complex, or book one of *Spiderwick Chronicles*, or short stories.

The Structure of the Lessons

Many of the lessons that follow are written out in their entirety. They follow a classic lesson architecture honed by Lucy Calkins in her *Units of Study* series, as a *connection* to introduce the lesson, a *teaching point* that names a reading skill, a *demonstration* in which we actually model that skill, usually naming smaller strategies and steps we follow, an *active engagement* where the kids get to try the work right there in the lesson, usually on a shared text we've already read together in read aloud, followed by a *link* that launches the kids into continuing the reading work in their own books. To fit all the lessons into this small book, though, sometimes I've given the teaching point—and then I'll give either the connection or link of the lesson, whichever seems more important to the tone and aim of the lesson. Sometimes how we lead into a lesson— the connection—really sets ups for kids *why* we might do this work. And sometimes our link—to their independent reading—really helps them understand *when* we might do this work and what it *looks like*. Of course, you can reinvent any of those parts, I simply wanted to give you some models that might help you envision the entire unit of study. Enjoy!

Yours,

Mary Ehrenworth

Analyzing the Setting for Its Physical and Psychological Implications

Getting Ready

- Have on hand a copy of *The Paper Bag Princess*, or any other concise, accessible fantasy story.

- You may choose to include film clips from fantasy movies or to introduce those in a prior read-aloud session.

- Read aloud the first chapter of *The Lightning Thief*—or the first chapter of whatever book you are reading aloud—in read-aloud, prior to this minilesson. *Deltora Quest* books are a good, shorter read-aloud. The *Spider-wick Chronicles* is an easier series of books. *Dragon Slayers' Academy* books are much easier and shorter. Riordan's *The Lost Hero* is newer.

▶ The aim of this lesson is to move students past identifying a setting with a word or a phrase (for example, it's the future, it's a place called Narnia) and into analyzing that place for its physical and psychological implications on the characters and the story. We hope that their analysis after this lesson will sound more like: "It's a place called Narnia, where power seems to be held by a White Witch, and everyone is afraid. Fear seeps through the land—and it's cold and wintery, which seems related to that fear." You'll want to practice analyzing and describing the places in the stories you've read, so you can demonstrate on some novels, as you teach and confer with the kids. You may also want to practice with some familiar movies, such as *Harry Potter*.

Connection

Stir up your readers—share your passion for this genre.

I had around me many gorgeous fantasy novels, their covers adorned with dragons, castles, and symbols. As I spoke, I gestured with these books. "Fantasy readers, today is the day when we start our unit of study in fantasy. Some of you are avid fantasy readers, I know. Others of you are a little unsure about this. You're not quite sure how you feel about dragons and dwarves and epic quests where the world is imperiled. Friends, let's begin, then, by thinking about *why* we would read fantasy. Here are some reasons. Reason one: because the stories are incredible. These are wild, dangerous, romantic tales, where the fate of mankind may rest on the choices made by the main character. Everything is more important, more intense, more vivid, in fantasy stories. Reason two: because when you study fantasy, really, you are studying the human condition. The stories are never really about elves and hobbits. They're about the struggle between good and evil, they're about how power corrupts, they're about the quest to be better than we are, they're about how even the smallest of us can affect what happens in this world. Reason three: because if you become a powerful reader of fantasy, you're likely to become a more powerful reader of all texts. Fantasy novels are incredibly complicated. You have to figure out where the story takes place, what kind of world it is, who has power there, what the rules are. You'll enter narratives that stretch over many novels; you'll read hundreds and even thousands of pages. You'll emerge, like the characters in these stories, changed."

"It's not accidental, friends, that the most widely read book in our lifetime is a story of a boy who finds he can do magic and how his life becomes an extraordinary quest to rid the world of evil. There is something transcendent about the very notion of Harry Potter. Who doesn't want to feel that your troubles are of extraordinary significance, to measure yourself against the heroes and villains of the ages, to forge bonds of friendship that will be tested by torture and by love? Four hundred million copies, translated into over sixty languages—it's a book that made the whole globe into a book club. If you read all seven novels, you read a story that spread over four thousand pages. You'll be reading in clubs that have fewer than four hundred million members, and I imagine you'll read fewer than four thousand pages together, but still, you get an idea of the epic quality of fantasy."

■ *You'll see here, that while our intention may be for our students to become adept at reading much more complicated stories, ones with multiple plotlines, complex characters, and unfamiliar settings, what we say is: fantasy! The lure of fantasy is a magical one.*

"I want that for you, friends. All of it: I want you to embark, from this classroom, with these friends, on wild adventures that make your head spin. I want you to feel the release that comes when you escape into other, mythic worlds where magic happens. I want you to find stories that spread over many books, that keep you up at night, and that fill the corners of your life with their secrets. You may or may not emerge from this study a fanatic—a Dungeons & Dragons player, a follower of Avatar, a reader of manga. But you will, I am sure, know more about this wild and beautiful genre. You will, I hope, have more insight into the human condition. And you will, I feel sure, emerge with an increased confidence that you can tackle truly complicated texts."

Name your teaching point. Specifically, teach your students that fantasy readers use multiple cuing systems to research the settings of their stories and the impact of the setting.

"Friends, today I want to teach you that fantasy readers understand that their first task is to figure out what kind of setting their story takes place in. Readers look for clues about the time period—and the magical elements, in particular—using the covers, blurbs, and details from the beginning of the story for their research. We know that the setting has physical and psychological implications on the character and the story."

Teaching

Explain some of the common settings of fantasy stories and demonstrate how you use this knowledge to research the setting of a shared text.

"Experienced fantasy readers expect certain kinds of places. Often, fantasy stories are set in a medieval world, full of swords, horses, castles, dragons, and so forth—like *The Lord of the Rings*, for instance, or *Narnia*. A second common setting is a futuristic world, full of spacecraft, intergalactic travel, and advanced technology—such as *Star Wars*. The third common setting is the ordinary world, where it seems at first as if everything is normal, but then gradually you notice an infiltration of magic, a kind of blending of the world we know with magical elements. *Harry Potter* is like this."

"Knowledgeable fantasy readers know to gather up clues, right away, about what kind of place they are in. Sometimes it's a little tricky, because the story might or might not begin right away in the magical world. *The Hobbit*, for instance, starts right off in a place full of creatures who grow to be only three feet tall, and they use carts and horses to farm, and there are wizards, so the reader knows that this place is magical. But other times, the story starts off in an ordinary place, in the here and now, and you think it's going to all happen here, and then the characters are transported. That's what happens in *Narnia:* Peter, Edmund, Lucy, and Susan all walk through an enchanted wardrobe into the magical kingdom of Narnia. In *Harry Potter,* Harry also starts off in the ordinary world, but that actual world becomes magical. He doesn't go to another kingdom. He still lives in London, in the modern world. But magic enters that world and transforms it."

■ *Teachers, you may show a few film clips from fantasy movies. The scenes give students a way to quickly compare multiple texts, and they bring all our readers, of any level, into this conversation. We can return later to look at issues of representation, gender norms, and critical literacy.*

"OK, readers, I've tried to jump-start your reading a bit here, as you can tell, by giving you a little expertise on how fantasy stories tend to start. That means I expect you, from the very first moment you begin reading, to be alert for details about what kind of place you encounter in the story you are reading. Things unfold rapidly in fantasy, and you have to get oriented quickly, before a dragon arrives or you get swept through a portal to another world."

"Watch how I do this work. I'm going to try to name what I do as a reader, as I do it, so you can see the steps I follow. Then you'll have a chance to practice on the story we read to-gether and, of course, afterward in the stories you'll read with your book clubs."

I picked up *The Paper Bag Princess.*

"OK, so . . . first, before I *even open the pages*, I look carefully at the covers of the book. I know that with the stories being this complicated, I want to get all the information I can from the covers. I'm looking to see if there's a blurb that might tell me who this story is about and, more important, what kind of world this is. . . . No! There is no blurb on this book. That doesn't seem fair. OK, next I'll look at the cover art and the title, as those can also tell me a lot. So . . . the book is called *The Paper Bag Princess*, and there is a girl with a bent crown, a huge castlelike door, and a gigantic, smoking dragon on the front cover. On the back cover is another image, of the same dragon breathing cataclysmic fire over the head of the girl. Hmm . . ."

I opened the inside of the book. "Inside, the story starts:"

Elizabeth was a beautiful princess. She lived in a castle and had expensive princess clothes. She was going to marry a prince named Ronald.

I looked at the page for a moment, saying, "And there's a picture of a snotty looking prince, with his nose in the air, and a besotted girl, staring at him with hearts flying around her. The room looks like a castle, with arched windows, stone walls, and old wooden chairs. And their clothes are definitely medieval (that's from the Middle Ages, like you'd see in the time of King Arthur). OK, so I definitely see from the furniture, the buildings, and the clothes that this story happens in a place that is medieval. On the next page, it says:"

Unfortunately, a dragon smashed her castle, burned all her clothes with his fiery breath, and carried off Prince Ronald.

"Aha! So there is magic here, too—this is not historical fiction, from the actual Middle Ages. A dragon has entered. That is definitely a magical creature. He has even magically managed to smash Elizabeth's castle and burn all of Elizabeth's clothes without harming her at all."

■ *In more complicated stories, the setting is literally setting up the reader. It incorporates both the mood or atmosphere and often some of the conflict for the character—it is definitely worth paying attention to! It might seem as if the setting in* The Paper Bag Princess *is simply some kind of place in the Middle Ages where there was a castle and a princess. But if you consider the psychological implications, it's more than that. It's a place where sudden violence happens. It's a place where no one is safe. It's a place where people are isolated and suddenly, often, alone.*

I put the book down. "OK, readers, I think I know enough. But what matters is that not only do I know about the physical time and place, but I'm getting a sense of what *kind* of place this is—its psychological implications. It seems pretty clear that this story begins in a place that is medieval. It has castles and old-fashioned clothes and princesses. And it is magical . . . there are dragons. There are *not* subways or laser guns or spacecraft. And, the story started right away in this magical kingdom. I know all this because I considered carefully what I learned from the pictures and text on the covers, the clues about daily life, and the appearance of any magic. It's also a place of sudden violence, where people's lives are ripped apart, and they can find themselves alone, facing horrid challenges without any support. It's a land that seems charming at first, but turns out to be unsafe."

Active Involvement

Look at your clues together.

"Readers, let's give you a chance to practice this work together. I'm going to return to the first chapter of *The Lightning Thief*. I saw when we were reading it that your jaws were practically hanging open as the story unfolded. Like me, you were entranced, and shocked, with how much happened and how wild it was. In fact, most of your conversation was simply retelling to each other what you *think* happened. You seemed as unsure as Percy was about what had really occurred on this field trip to the Metropolitan Museum. It didn't help that at the end of the first chapter, after Percy Jackson's teacher has turned into a demon and tried to *kill* him in the middle of the museum, that his favorite teacher, Mr. Brunner, apparently denies that any of it even happened."

I picked up *The Lightning Thief*. "Friends, we dove right into the story, so that everything happened fast and without any warning. When Mrs. Dodds suddenly turned into a demon, it was pretty confusing. This time, let's see if we could have gathered more clues a little earlier. Then we'd have a deeper understanding of what kind of place Percy is living in."

I held the book up so that everyone could see it. "Readers, I'm going to show you the covers, and read you what's on the back blurb. This time, follow my example in using the strategy of really researching the time period and the magical elements within the story by paying extra attention to the covers and the start of the story."

"So, on the cover is an image of New York City, seen from the water. Lightning crackles down past the Empire State Building. It's dark and stormy. Emerging from the ocean, apparently dry even though he comes up out of the deep waves, is a dark-haired boy. He holds in one hand some kind of object."

Turn and Talk

■ *You'll notice, teachers, that I'm giving the kids a couple of opportunities to turn and talk during this session. That's because I want students to notice details and have a chance to analyze them before those details are replaced by the next set of details. So I've broken their partner talks into two parts here. Also, invite readers who have already read the book to partner together, so they'll have new insights. If you're reading a different novel, such as* The Hunger Games, *that doesn't have such a riveting cover, you can still ponder the possible significance of the title and image—or have on hand a few fantasy novels to practice with.*

"Friends, I can tell you have a lot to say already about the clues that a reader could gather here about what kind of place this is, before he or she even opens the book. Turn and tell your partner all of what you might surmise, just from the cover so far."

They did. I jotted some notes. Then I summarized their conversations: "Pause for a moment, friends, and I'll share some of what you are saying. A lot of you spoke about how it is clearly modern times, because you can see New York City landmarks, such as the Empire State Building. Many of you described the kid's clothes as being contemporary, which is another clue that it's here and now. But then you spoke of the glowing sword and the way the kid emerges from the waves as being magical. It's not as if you normally see kids with glowing swords, who can walk through oceans and not get wet, on Fifth Avenue. I love, as well, how some of you said that it seems like a violent place—it's dark and ominous. It seems threatening."

"This is good, you're really researching thoughtfully. I'm going to show you the back cover next, because that would be your next strategy. Let's see how that helps your research. I imagine that you'd want to jot down notes. If you were doing this with your club book or your independent reading book, I'd definitely expect that you'd know to make a quick notebook entry so you'd hold onto your research. When you read harder books like this, you definitely want to use all your strategies to jump-start your reading from a more knowledgeable place."

■ *Students can jot as you read, and you may read it twice. I read the two opening paragraphs, from "Percy Jackson is about to be kicked out of boarding school" to "unravel a treachery more powerful than the gods themselves." This and the start of Riordan's* The Last Hero *have to be among the most riveting first few pages of any young adult novel.*

Turn and Talk

I put the book down. "Whoa, I can't believe how much better prepared we would have been as readers if we had read this first! I could see you jotting furiously. Turn and tell your partner about the research this blurb would help you with."

They did. I jotted what they said.

I pulled them back and shared some of their conversations. "Readers, I heard you say that from the blurb, our research tells us that Percy lives in the modern world. He goes to boarding school, he reads textbooks, and he studies Greek mythology. But you also said that you found out that there is dark magic in this world: it seems that the Greek myths are, in fact, real. Zeus is one of the characters. There is an Oracle. And a magic lightning bolt. And monsters. It's an unsafe place and clearly Percy will be threatened by this dark magic."

I looked at our notes. Then I said, "Well, readers, we certainly found that this research paid off, didn't we? Our next strategy would be to reread the first part of the book and see if there were any clues that we might have picked up, because we now know that there is magic in this modern world."

■ *You can read the first part now, or simply let them retell and recall for a moment. They'll have more ideas about things they should have realized if they knew that this place was magical.*

Link

Send your students off, reminding them to research the settings as they begin their stories.

I put down *The Lightning Thief,* saying, "Friends, this work is going to be very important now for you as readers. The novels you're choosing are complicated. The places will be unusual and significant, and you'll want to use the strategies you know to be alert to details about these places and their physical and psychological implications. So, not just today, but whenever you pick up a complex novel, you'll want to research the place carefully, using the covers, the blurb, and all the details in the beginning of the story. Off you go, readers. I'll be eager to see you do this work and listen to your conversations when you'll have a chance to share your research on the stories you are reading."

■ *One thing that is really interesting about reading strategies is that after using them ritualistically for a time, you may move to a stage where you think you don't need them so much, as you become more confident with some levels of text. Most of my teen readers now ignore the information from the covers, beyond how it entices them to choose the book. But the truth is that often, as you tackle even more complicated texts, you need those strategies again. That's what I hope we convey to students in this lesson as well: their repertoire will be cyclical in terms of how much and how often they use various strategies. It's not that you learn one strategy, master it, use it all the time, or then never need it as you learn new strategies. It's more that you turn to your repertoire depending on what kind of reading work you're doing and what your relationship to the book is.*

Understanding Cuing Systems in Complex Novels

Learning Alongside the Main Character

Getting Ready

▶ Read through Chapter Three in *The Lightning Thief*, or through enough of whatever novel you are reading that the character has started to have some realizations: he or she is on a learning quest as well as an adventure, and there are usually obvious spots where the character learns important information about this magical realm. Stay alert to those spots so you can teach your readers to learn alongside the character.

▶ Have *The Paper Bag Princess* on hand. I'm assuming you've read this in a prior read-aloud. It takes about ten or twenty minutes to read the whole story.

You'll also want to start some kind of visual timeline, a character list, and perhaps a map of your read-aloud text so that you can jot pivotal moments, remember characters, and locate important places. Ask kids to help create these, and just casually add to them during and after your read-aloud, as an implicit model of how to use a reading notebook to deepen our understanding of complex novels.

Connection

Tell a story about your reading experience, where a main character seems confused by his or her environment.

Teachers, one thing that happens in harder fantasy—and historical fiction—is that the author often tries to help the reader by giving information through the mouths of characters. You'll note, for instance, that a character asks about a legend or a historical incident, and an experienced reader knows to think, "Aha! I'm supposed to pay attention here. Anytime that character describes some incident, legend, or history, you're supposed to learn about it, too. Tumnus tells Lucy about Narnia. Gandalf tells Frodo about the history of the ring of power. Dumbledore tells Harry about Voldemort's history. Alert readers sit up at these times and take mental notes. Or sometimes the main character has a dramatic, explicit learning experience. He comes away with new realizations, and we are supposed to, too. We're on the same learning curve as the main character. Give some vivid examples of how main characters are on a learning

*journey as well as a quest, and explain how the reader is
supposed to learn alongside those characters.*

*Name your teaching point. Specifically, teach your
students that fantasy readers expect to learn alongside
the main character and are alert to clues that characters
are in the midst of important learning experiences.*

"Readers, today I want to teach you that in complicated stories such as these fantasy novels, the main characters often
begin without a lot of knowledge, and they have a steep
learning curve. When the main character is told important information or has dramatic new experiences, alert readers see
those moments in the story as opportunities not just for the
character to learn but for themselves to learn hand-in-hand
with the main character."

Teaching

*Demonstrate in your read-aloud text how you learn
with the main characters as they ask questions,
hear explanations, and have new experiences.*

"Let me show you what this looks like, friends. I see you reading *Dragon Slayers' Academy* and *Harry Potter* books and *The
Lion, the Witch and the Wardrobe,* so I know this will help you.
In the stories you are reading—indeed, in most fantasy
stories—often the main characters are outsiders. Wiglaf
doesn't know much about Dragon Slayers' Academy, Harry

doesn't know much about magic or Hogwarts, and Lucy definitely doesn't know much about Narnia at the beginning. And so, these characters are not only on an adventure quest, they're also on a learning journey."

"Often, readers, characters in fantasy stories go to new places as they embark on quests or journeys. That means they have a lot of opportunities to learn about these places. In a way, by making the characters a little ignorant, the author helps us learn. Instead of being frustrated that our main characters aren't more expert, we can try to build our expertise at the same pace that they do. We listen for when characters ask questions, we pay attention to the answers they get, and we try to learn rapidly."

■ *Interestingly, when readers take in the information from the back covers of their stories, they often begin the story knowing more than the main character does. In a way, that lets us read with a kind of bird's-eye view, alert to those learning opportunities that will bring the main character along his or her learning curve.*

"Readers, I've read a lot of fantasy, so I expect that I have to learn alongside the main character. I don't get frustrated if things seem confusing at the start, and I try to be extra alert to moments when the main characters ask questions, listen to explanations, or have new learning experiences. I need to read those moments almost like a nonfiction reader would, keeping files in my mind (or in my notes) about what I learn. In more complicated stories, you'll notice that often the main character has a pretty steep learning curve that we're supposed to join in on."

"Let me show you what this looks like. Basically, I want to show you how there are certain moments in the story in which you can almost feel the author saying to you, 'Listen up, this matters!' Often those moments are marked by the main characters visibly trying to learn. Sometimes their learning isn't totally successful: in complicated stories it takes a long time to learn everything. But it's as if you can see them *trying* to learn."

"For instance, let's go back to Chapter Two. Watch how alert I am to anytime the main character asks direct questions or gets to hear any kind of explanations. Percy had just returned to school with Mr. Brunner, Grover, and the other students, after the incident where he was, he thinks, attacked by Mrs. Dodds. He is confused. Readers, Percy is definitely not an insider yet in this world. Just like Lucy in Narnia, Harry at Hogwarts, and Wiglaf at DSA, Percy has so much to learn. And then there is this moment when Percy overhears Mr. Brunner asking Grover questions about Percy."

■ *I motioned to our continuing timeline. You'll want a timeline going alongside your read-aloud. I point to an event that I have on the timeline: Percy overhears Mr. Brunner and Grover talking about him.*

"Readers, recall that I said that experienced readers expect to be extra alert to anytime the character asks questions, hears explanations, or has new learning experiences?" I ticked these off on my fingers. Then I went on, "Well, in all of Chapter Two, Percy is confused about what is going on, about what's real or not, and it means we're uncertain, too.

Then there is this moment when he eavesdrops on Mr. Brunner and Grover. Grover is explaining why he is worried about Percy."

■ *I go back to the book here, and reread aloud the part where Percy suddenly finds himself learning a lot—almost too much for him to take in and comprehend, which is common with characters who begin their journeys in ignorance. It's on pages 19–20 of my edition, which is just two pages or so into Chapter Two. In any book, though, until the main characters have more experiences, and sometimes until they know more about themselves as well, they can't really make sense of all the new information coming at them. It's important for readers to realize that they learn alongside the characters, and also that they sometimes learn at an even faster rate than the characters. If you're reading a different book, start with a spot where it's clear that there is new information being conveyed.*

I reread the line:

Mr. Brunner asked a question. A voice that was definitely Grover's said, ". . . worried about Percy, sir."
    I froze.

I repeated that last line and added: "I did too, readers, I froze! Just as Percy expected to learn something important in this moment, I, too, expected to learn. Let's look at what came next."

Now I reread the next few paragraphs, from "I'm not usually an eavesdropper" to "Mr. Brunner went silent."

I put down the book and paused. "Readers, you'll remember that Percy was shaken by what he overheard. He went back to his dorm room, where he lay awake, trying to figure out all these things that he knew he didn't understand. That was a signal to me to figure things out, too. Just as Percy probably replayed this conversation in his head, I reread it several times. As I did, several things became clear. I'll show you my notes."

I put my notebook page on the overhead. On it I had jotted:

> I wonder if the "Kindly One" in school is Mrs. Dodds? And also, it seems as if Percy is in danger. There's a deadline of summer solstice. I'm worried about him because he seems so "ignorant," just like Mr. Brunner said! Also, I think the "Mist" convinces people that they haven't seen things. And Grover knows more than Percy, because Grover feels he failed to see Mrs. Dodds for what she was. I hope Percy figures this all out.

"Readers, do you see how I was extra alert as soon as I realized this was an important learning opportunity for Percy? I could tell that a conversation like this would probably reveal important new information, so I was ready to learn. I may even have learned more than Percy did! That's actually a really cool moment in a story, when you realize that the author is giving you clues and that you are inferring ahead of the character. What matters is that as soon as I realized that a significant conversation was about to happen, I was alert and ready, which is why I now know so much more."

Active Involvement

Remind students of text markers that indicate pivotal moments in a character's learning curve, such as direct questions, explanations, and unfamiliar experiences, and set them up to try this work on a text excerpt of the read-aloud.

"Readers, what often happens is that as the story moves along, there are fast parts and slower parts and parts where it's almost all action. There are parts like the one I just reread, where it's pretty much all conversation. Those moments are often pivotal ones in a character's learning curve. I hope you see that readers expect to learn something from conversations, especially any conversations the main character overhears or ones in which direct questions are posed. In a fast-moving story like *The Lightning Thief*, important conversations take place even in the middle of action. But if you see the main character asking direct questions, listening to explanations or stories, or having new, unfamiliar experiences, you know you should be alert to learn alongside the character during those pivotal moments."

I jotted on the chart paper:

Pivotal moments in characters' learning curves
- Direct questions and answers
- Explanations or stories
- Unfamiliar experiences

"Let's give this a try. I'm going to read the next part of the story, which is Chapter Four. So far, we've mostly been adding to our timeline of events as we read during read-aloud and talking about the characters, as we would at the start of any story. This time, though, can you be extra alert to any clues such as the ones I just jotted, and be ready to tell your partner about the moments when you learned at the same time that Percy visibly learned something new? We'll start right after where we finished, which was just as Grover appeared at the summer cottage where Percy and his mother were staying. Grover was frantic. And he had hooves."

■ *Teachers, you'll want to choose an excerpt that you've already read aloud, so that students can ponder the new information that is given in this excerpt and not just be on the edge of their seats, wanting you to read on for the action. I picked up the story where we had left off, which is Chapter Four: "My Mother Teaches Me Bullfighting." I read from the first line, "We tore through the night along dark country roads," until Grover explains, "We hoped you'd think the Kindly One was a hallucination. But it was no good. You started to realize who you are." I chose this excerpt because Grover explicitly tries to teach Percy—he offers him explanations of prior experiences. Investigate whatever novel or short text you're reading aloud and you'll find these moments. They occur in most complex narratives.*

Turn and Talk—and then Summarize

■ *If you actually call on the kids to share their insights after having already given them time to talk in partnerships and build on those insights, you'll be in the lesson forever. I listen to the kids while they talk in partnerships, take notes, and then share some of their insights. This method lets you add on to their practices as well.*

I looked up. "Wow, readers, I could see you taking lots of notes. Every time Percy asked a question, I saw you pick up your pencils. That's what I mean, friends, about being alert to the questions and explanations. Why don't you compare your learning with what your partner learned in this part?"

They did.

I summarized some of what they said. "Friends, many of you gathered a lot of information about satyrs in this part, and, like Percy, you realized that Grover is, in fact, a satyr. Some of you took more notes on the Mist as well. We seem to be finding out that it produces some kind of hallucination. Percy learned all of that in this section, and I'm pleased to see that you were alert, ready to learn at Percy's side. And a few of you noted that Grover said that Percy attracts monsters. Hmm . . . that might be useful to know! I wonder if Percy caught that? Sometimes, there is this odd thing that happens, when you realize that maybe you caught even more from a conversation than the main character did."

Link

Give your students a moment to talk about the learning curve of the main character in their book. Then encourage your students to keep alert and to perhaps use their pencils as they read, and send them off.

"Before we go off to read, friends, take a moment to tell your partner about the learning curve of your main character. Is your character far along on this learning curve or just getting started? You'll have a chance to do lots of thinking about the character's learning as you read, but this conversation will help you figure out if the character's learning curve reflects yours. I look forward to hearing more of your conversations later. You may find it useful to jot some notes or to flag parts of your novel as you read, to keep track of these pivotal moments and their implications. Off you go."

Disentangling Complicated Narratives

Getting Ready

▶ Read *The Lightning Thief* through Chapter Nine or the next part of your read-aloud text.

▶ Bring a transcript of a club conversation and a sample chart. You could prompt a club to create this work beforehand, so that you can display it today in your teaching.

Connection

Tell a personal story about a time when problems began to multiply.

■ *Teachers, I tell a story about how I set out to solve one problem in my life, and the problems kept multiplying. I use an example of how I set out to rescue some kittens, only to have them immediately develop life-threatening emergencies that led to late-night traumas, then once they were healed and home, I realized I was allergic. It was a sequence of solving one problem and then facing another— but learning that you can, in fact, keep solving problems. You could also describe how at the end of the first* Harry Potter *novel, Harry does find the sorcerer's stone. But when he found it, he also found Lord Voldemort, who was released from his years of not having a body and became a sort of evil spirit who would come back in the next book. So Harry solved one problem, only to have another arise. However, he becomes stronger each time he finds he has to rise to face new problems. If your students are reading books at and above level R-S-T, chances are that the stories they are reading have multiple plotlines and unresolved problems. This work is crucial to that described by the Common Core Standards: the ability to analyze complex texts at high levels.*

Name your teaching point. Specifically, teach your students that complicated stories have multiple plot-lines and problems. One way to keep track of the characters, problems, and storylines is to use charts, timelines, and other graphic organizers that help you gather evidence so that you can be more analytical as a reader and a thinker.

"Friends, as you tackle more complicated books, the stories begin to have multiple plotlines. This means that the main characters have more than one problem, that problems arise for other characters, and that not all problems are resolved by the end of a story. Often readers find it helpful to use charts, timelines, and other graphic organizers to track the problems that arise in a story to closely follow the multiple plotlines and to gather evidence the way scientists do, in charts and tables that let us do close analysis."

Teaching

Share a transcript of a club conversation that demonstrates the many problems that arise, and aren't all solved, in complex stories.

"Readers, yesterday I was listening to Sam, Jose, and Michael talk about the end of the first book in the series they're reading together—*The New Kid at School*, part of the *Dragon Slayers' Academy* series. I got so intrigued by their conversation that I wrote it down. I think that it illustrates one of the issues found in more complicated stories—that there will be more than one problem. I'm going to put the transcript of their conversation up here. Can you put on your reading researcher lenses and see what this conversation suggests to you about the notion of multiple plotlines and problems? You might want to do some jotting, so I'm glad you've got your notebooks."

I put the transcript up for students to see:

MICHAEL: I can't believe Wiglaf killed the dragon!
    JOSE: I know! That was all he wanted—to kill a dragon so he could get gold for his family.

SAM: But now headmaster Mordred has stolen his gold anyway! So he killed the dragon for nothing.

MICHAEL: I know . . . and he feels bad about it, too. Now Wiglaf has a new problem: he doesn't like killing dragons.

SAM: But the dragons don't know that. And I notice the next book is called *Revenge of the Dragon Lady*.

MICHAEL: Well, that's a new problem for Wiglaf.

JOSE: So the book ends and Wiglaf is still poor. And now he has a new problem: he's at a school for dragon slayers, and he's a dragon-liker. And the dragons hate him.

MICHAEL: And what about Wiglaf's friend, Eric? When is he going to impress everyone? He's so desperate to kill a dragon, but it was Wiglaf who did it.

SAM: Actually, Eric's problem is that he's a girl. Wiglaf is a secret dragon-liker, and Eric is secretly a girl. I read ahead. Her problem is worse than Wiglaf's. And it stays worse for longer. And Angus has problems, too. He's Mordred's nephew. That stinks. And he can't stay away from sweets.

JOSE: At least Mordred's happy, because he has gold now.

MICHAEL: Nah, Mordred will always want more gold. You can tell. He's greedy, and greedy people are never satisfied.

JOSE: Snap! These folks have a lot of problems.

Turn and Talk

"Readers, I see you have some notes and ideas. Why don't you turn to your partner and share your research. What did you notice about the issue of multiple plotlines and problems? Turn and talk."

■ *Clearly, teachers, this transcript closely matches the teaching point. A hint: set up some students to produce the kind of teaching tool you think might be useful to your class. You might gather a club and do some preteaching beforehand, and then transcribe some of their work.*

They talked. I gathered them back.

"Readers, it's kind of amazing, isn't it, how much is happening in the *Dragon Slayers' Academy* book, how many plotlines and problems arise? And we definitely saw that by the end of the story, only some problems were resolved. Michael, Jose, and Sam are having some rich conversation about the different conflicts in their first book."

"Readers, I recommended that they invent some kind of chart or other graphic organizer to keep track of the problems that arose in the book, and how those problems are solved or change, or which new ones arise across the book and even into the next book in the series. Let me show you one simple chart that this club invented."

I put up the chart in Figure 3.1.

■ *Teachers, you can imagine that we could teach our readers that it might be helpful to do separate charts for separate characters, once they have this much information. The main point, though, is that to analyze evidence, you need to collect it, just as they do in their science labs. Analytical thinking comes from paying attention to detail. Resist the urge, though, to make a handout. Readers should invent their own tools, and those tools should be malleable. Once you make something, it is in danger of becoming an assignment.*

"Readers, I can imagine how this quick chart would really launch a long and deeply analytical conversation, can't you?

Character	Problem	Solution / Change	By the End
Wiglaf	Needs gold	Kills a dragon	Mordred takes the gold
Eric	Wants to impress everyone by killing a dragon	Goes with Wiglaf and finds dragon	Can't figure out how to kill dragon; Wiglaf gets the glory
Mordred	Wants gold	Sends students to kill dragons	Takes Wiglaf's gold
Eric	Is a girl	Dresses as a boy	Still hasn't told anyone
Wiglaf	Was poor	Can't keep gold	Still poor
All the DSA students	Mordred bullies them	None	None—he still bullies them, and he steals from them
Wiglaf	Wants to kill a dragon	Kills a dragon	Finds out he hates killing dragons; also dragons want revenge

FIG. 3.1

These quick charts and timelines are great starting places for detailed conversations. They don't take long to invent—it's not that much writing—but they help us make our book club conversations more substantial because we've done so much collecting and have created opportunities for real thinking."

Active Involvement

Bring your students to a recent chapter of the read-aloud text to practice this work. Begin keeping public records/charts to support the read-aloud.

"Readers, we've been keeping a timeline of the big events in *The Lightning Thief* as we read. But I'm not sure that's enough.

A lot is going on in this story. We're at Chapter Nine now. Let's just consider, not what's happened but how many problems we can name, for Percy and/or his friends. Let's try that for a moment. Turn to your partner, and jot down all the problems that you can discern so far in this story. Use whatever method you want to keep track of those problems. I'll try to catch what you're saying and jot it up here."

Turn and Talk

■ *As they talked, I played up that they had so many details flying around that it was impossible to really collect and compare them without gathering them in some kind of organized fashion.*

"Whoa, readers, I'm going to interrupt you. It's too hard for me to catch everything! I've jotted that Percy doesn't know for sure who his father is. Then later one of you said he finds out who his father is—it's Poseidon—but Percy is upset that his father doesn't contact him. Then I heard one of you say that another problem is that Clarisse hates Percy. But someone else said that Clarisse's problem is that her dad, Ares, is a jerk. Then someone said that Percy has a problem because he can't talk to Annabeth. But someone else said that Percy's problem is his mother has been killed, and he has to rescue her from the underworld . . ."

"Yikes! Readers, this story is so complicated, with so many problems emerging for so many characters, that it will be helpful to organize a little writing to keep track of these problems and how they change, as the Dragon Slayers' Academy club did. Why don't you start this work now, in your notebook, and we'll use it to begin our next conversation in read-aloud. I can imagine that you might start a chart that is just Percy's problems, or you might include Annabeth and Grover. Or you might envision some other kind of timeline or graphic organizer that would capture this thinking across the book. You'll have your own particular method for capturing your analysis. Why don't you sketch out something, and begin it for a minute to practice this work and help us prepare for our next read-aloud?"

They began to create charts and timelines in their notebooks.

▩ *Teachers, you may want to gather some of the charts and timelines and any other useful tools the students invent, and make copies to put up alongside the writing you've been doing along with the read-aloud, to provide examples of mentor "writing about reading" for your kids. Particularly push kids to write reflections or captions under their charts, so that they demonstrate the move from gathering evidence to analytical thinking.*

Link

Reflect on how you'll use these charts and graphic organizers for your own reading and book club conversations, and send your students off to do the same.

▩ *Your students will love to hear about and see the work that you are doing for your book club. It gives an authentic tone* to the book club work you ask them to do. Anytime you can start or end a lesson with "you know, in my book club . . ." you truly speak as a mentor reader. Tell your students about your own upcoming work, encourage them to invent their own tools, and send them off.

Reading Notebooks Deepen Our Engagement and Analytical Thinking

Preparing for Partner Conversations and Book Clubs

Getting Ready

▶ Tell your readers at least a day or two in advance that you'll be sharing favorite pages from their reading notebooks. Give them some time in class to revise or extend what they've done so far in preparation. Have colored pencils on hand to add to their engagement. A note: some readers may keep digital notebooks. Increasingly, the notebook is a metaphor for wherever we write.

- Have on hand the charts, timelines, and maps that support your read-aloud text.

- This lesson is set up as an inquiry, not as a traditional minilesson. Students will lay their notebook on their desks, open to their favorite or most significant pages. Then they'll do a "gallery walk," which is when they walk around, taking notes, sometimes leaving sticky notes for the author, and sharing practices.

- In classrooms where I see kids doing the most productive, perceptive, and fluent writing about reading—including making on-the-run charts, diagrams, and visuals, as well as longer reflections—the teacher is doing this work, too, usually in a demonstration reading notebook. They do what we *do*, not what we tell them to do!

Teaching Point and Introduction to the Gallery Walk/Inquiry

"Readers, today I want to teach you that experienced readers have a repertoire of writing-about-reading strategies that we mine to deepen our engagement with literature and to support our reading work and our conversations. These include making visuals, sorting and analyzing sticky notes and entries, experimenting with charts and flowcharts, and writing reflections. One way to extend this repertoire is for a learning community to share with each other the different ways that we use our notebooks as we read. Today we're going to share our practices by doing a gallery walk. That's where we each put out our notebooks, open to some favorite or significant pages. As we walk around the room, readers can examine these pages for new ideas. None us simply knows enough or has invented all the creative ways that readers can use writing to deepen their engagement with books. You might call out praise or invite the author to explain his or her techniques. You might leave a sticky note admiring something specific. Most important, your goal is to return to your desk ready to tell your partner about a few new ideas you have for your own writing about reading."

■ *Teachers, during the gallery walk, model being an avid learner and participant. You'll ask a student to explain a chart, and then try that chart using the read-aloud text, giving credit to its inventor. I keep a demonstration reading notebook, much like my writer's notebook, that I use to model with kids. It used to be on paper. This year it's on my iPad. The Penultimate app works well as it is a digital notebook and you can write with a stylus.*

At the end of the gallery walk and after partners have had a chance to talk and share new ideas for their notebooks, ask students to call out favorite pages they saw in others' notebooks. This chart might help some readers when they are unsure when and how it's worth it to do some jotting as they read (see Figure 4.1). As adults, we remember when we first tried a Russian novel and had to jot the characters' names inside the cover. Or we'll go get a map and tuck it into the memoir we are reading of the child soldier in Africa. Our students need us to model and promote those reading practices.

To Hold onto the Story	To Deepen Our Engagement
Character lists, charts, and webs	Writing long about reflections
Charts of problems, solutions, change	Poems inspired by the story
Timelines of events, emotions	Illustrations of significant moments
Maps	Descriptions of lasting images
Setting descriptions and illustrations	Charts of other titles and characters, so we can compare across books
Quick jottings about responses	
Writing about predictions and theories	Writing long about themes and lessons
Pictorial glossaries	Quoting and celebrating craft
Facts and information sections	Writing like the author, or inspired by the story

FIG. 4.1 *Some Writing About Reading Techniques*

A possible chart might end up with some of these examples. Make some color copies of great kids' pages and put them up as examples, or keep a blog or an online collection. The more often you do these gallery walks (we did them every Friday) and the more kids' work is public, celebrated, and influential, the more rigorous they become in their work habits.

Here Be Dragons

Thinking Metaphorically About the Problems Characters Struggle With

Getting Ready

▶ Have *The Paper Bag Princess* on hand.

▶ Read through the end of Chapter Twelve in *The Lightning Thief*, or through the next big section of your read-aloud text.

▶ You could bring in or upload an image of the Carta Marina to show your students. It has sea monsters attacking ships in places the mariners considered dangerous. The Lenox Globe, of which there are also zillions of online images, was the first map to include the phrase "Here Be Dragons."

- If, in the previous lesson, you or the students made some charts of the many problems that characters face in *The Lightning Thief,* it would be helpful to have those on hand.

- Have on hand an excerpt from your read-aloud text that gives evidence for the big emotional conflicts, or "dragons," that characters struggle with. We use an excerpt from pages 191–192. You could show this on chart paper or on a screen, or you could photocopy it.

Connection

Share a story that demonstrates metaphor, such as the "Here Be Dragons" term on old maps, which symbolized the host of unknown dangers that travelers might encounter.

"Readers, have you ever seen old maps from the first mariners who charted the oceans? I love these charts because they are so gorgeous and mysterious and symbolic. When they wanted to show that someplace was dangerous, for instance, they might write "Here Be Dragons" on that area. The Latin words for that, *Hic Sunt Dracones*, were first written on a famous globe called the Lenox Globe, from around 1510."

"The cartographers might also show sea monsters lurking along the coast. A really beautiful map that I adore, called the Carta Marina, was created in the sixteenth century. It shows dragons attacking boats and all the mythical dangers one would encounter if you ever dared to leave the familiar shores of your homeland." (See Figure 5.1.)

"Readers, what's fascinating about these charts is that the dragons and sea monsters on them are symbolic. Yes, long ago, mariners probably saw giant squid and then pictured them on their maps as sea monsters. But mapmakers also put dragons on maps to show that a place was unknown and dangerous. They showed dragons where earthquakes happened. They marked the borders of unknown terrain with *Hic Sunt Dracones.* 'Here Be Dragons' has come to be a symbolic expression that means 'look out, you're in dangerous territory—don't go there.'"

Name your teaching point. Specifically, teach your students that some of the dragons that characters face are metaphoric dragons. One way readers explore these "dragons" is to consider the inner struggles that characters face.

"Readers, today I want to teach you that in the stories you are reading, the characters face dragons as well. Not just literal dragons, which some fantasy characters do encounter, but metaphoric dragons: these are the conflicts inside a character's soul that haunt that character. Powerful readers learn to think metaphorically about these 'dragons.'"

FIG. 5.1 *A small section of the Carta Marina*

Teaching

Demonstrate the difference between real dragons and metaphoric dragons. Foster the idea that all characters have dragons.

"Let's go back to a favorite story to illustrate this thinking."

I picked up *The Paper Bag Princess*. "Remember *The Paper Bag Princess*? Well, in this book, Elizabeth literally faces a dragon. When I think about the big problem that Elizabeth has, it's that a dragon has smashed her castle and taken Prince Ronald away. Of course, Elizabeth conquers this dragon. She finds the dragon, tricks him, and exhausts him, and she completes her quest by rescuing Prince Ronald."

"But readers, *The Paper Bag Princess* is a more complicated story than just this simple quest. If all that happened was that Elizabeth rescued Prince Ronald, there wouldn't be any significant character change and the story wouldn't be that memorable for us. But Elizabeth does change. She has a second huge, important, life-changing moment, when she faces up to something hard, something as hard or harder than the flame-breathing monster she has already conquered."

"When she gets to that cave and rescues Ronald, Elizabeth finds that Ronald is just as much of a monster as the dragon was. At least the dragon was respectful, even if he did want to eat her. Ronald turns out to be monstrously cruel. 'Elizabeth,' he says, when she has finally made her way through danger and death, through burned forests and fields of horses' bones, to this cave, 'you are a mess! You smell like ashes, your hair is all tangled and you are wearing a dirty old paper bag. Come back when you are dressed like a real princess.'"

"Readers, I come to this part of the story, and here's what I think. I think: 'Aha! *Hic Sunt Dracones!* Here be dragons! This is Elizabeth's real dragon! Ronald is her dragon—he's the thing that she needs to conquer. He's the problem she has to get past. His cruelty and indifference, his snobbery, his way of ignoring, demeaning, and humiliating her—that's her dragon. If I were a medieval cartographer making a map of this story, I would show Ronald as a dragon to symbolize his monstrous nature."

■ *Teachers, this is a powerful move to make as a reader, to begin to think metaphorically. It's one reason that I love to start any year, any grade, with* The Paper Bag Princess. *There is something about the literalness of the dragon imagery, the way it symbolizes danger, that seems to help young readers move into metaphoric thinking gracefully. Ask your kids about the dragons in their lives and see what stories emerge. It turns into great writing workshop work as well.*

"Do you see how I did this, readers? I thought *metaphorically*. I moved to thinking about dragons not as real but as *metaphoric* dragons that characters face. When you do this, readers, you can begin to think deeply about the dragons in all characters' lives and in our own lives as well. Ask yourself, for a moment: What are your dragons?" I paused, as if considering my own dragons. "I have a few, readers. You'll know them from writing workshop. My friend, Audra Robb, talks often of how, across the many years of our lives, we'll tend to write about the same issues, the same themes . . . the same dragons. It's a provocative question to ask, isn't it? What are your dragons?"

"Now watch me as I try applying this way of thinking—of thinking metaphorically about the dragons that characters face—to *The Lightning Thief*. I say to myself: I bet Percy Jackson has dragons in his life, big issues that haunt him that he needs to get past. That's how you think about this, readers. You think about the things that characters need to get past; it's like an internal quest that characters are on. So I don't mean small stuff, like when Percy wants to do well on his mythology final exam. I'm talking about the big emotional conflicts that are Percy's dragons."

I picked up the book and then looked at our timeline of events and some of the charts we had produced in earlier lessons, about the multiple problems the characters in this story face. Then I said, "Friends, I'm thinking back over all the problems we've been talking about. Just looking at some of our timelines and charts, for instance, I'm reminded of the monsters Percy faces, like the Minotaur who kills his mother. That incident caused another problem in Percy's life—how to get his mother back from the underworld—which leads to all sorts of related problems. Hmm . . . let me see if I can group some of these problems together, or if any of them become emotional conflicts, rather than real, physical monsters. So, I'm letting go of the actual monsters and focusing on the metaphoric ones. . . . "

I thought a little longer. "Well, when I think metaphorically, I guess, after Percy's mother is killed by the Minotaur, it feels like one of Percy's dragons is the guilt he feels about her death. All he wants is to get her back, to get rid of this feeling. This emotion colors all his actions. It makes him secretive with his friends. It drives his actions. Yes, this guilt feels to me like one of Percy's dragons."

Active Involvement

Give your readers a chance to try thinking metaphorically about characters' dragons, in the read-aloud text and/or their own stories.

"Readers, do you see how I pushed myself to think metaphorically, considering what big emotional conflicts the character struggles with? I asked myself: What are Percy's dragons? What haunts him, what does he need to get past, what drives him? To do this work, I considered all the charts and timelines, all the notes I've made so far about the multiple problems characters face, all the reading work I've done so far about characters' conflicts, and this time I tried to analyze the emotional aspect of these problems."

"Let's give you a chance to try this work, readers. One way to do this thinking is to look back over your notes and to reconsider the many problems that a character faces. Then see if some of these issues add up to a big emotional 'dragon'— a place in the character's emotional life where you might say 'here be dragons!' You might be able to do this for Annabeth or Grover as well as for Percy, as we've done so much work recently, charting the multiple problems that become visible in complicated stories like this. Use all your materials, readers, and when you begin to have some ideas, turn and talk with your partner."

They did.

■ *Teachers, you'll find that any public records you've made, such as charts and timelines of the multiple plotlines and problems in your read-aloud text, are incredibly helpful. Having tools at hand that help us to recall important parts of the story means that students can move more easily from recall work to thinking deeply about characters.*

After partners had been working and talking for a few minutes, I called them back. "Readers, I heard some fascinating conversations. Clearly it's productive to ask the question: What are this character's dragons? Some of you focused on Annabeth, and I heard you say that her relationship with her dad is her dragon. She seems haunted by it, every time it comes up. Others of you talked about Grover, and how he seems to have some secret dragon that we don't totally understand yet. He often mentions that something terrible happened on his first quest, but we don't know more because every time he mentions it, he says that he can't talk about it! I love the way you're uncovering dragons that are kind of lurking behind corners. And Percy seems to have a few dragons, right? Some of you talked more about his guilt. Others of you talked about his feelings about his father, that he seems to feel abandoned and that makes him want to prove himself."

■ *Sometimes, when young readers start developing exciting theories, they stop using the text as evidence for those theories. They love the new language they are acquiring;*

they like the sense of intellectual headiness that comes
with this kind of grand thinking work. Next, therefore, we'll
show them how to zoom in on a part of the story and gather
details to support their thinking.

I picked up the book again. "Readers, I want to show you one more thing, since you're doing this incredible thinking. Sometimes, when you are thinking metaphorically like this, it's helpful to ground your thinking in specific moments in the text. For instance, look for places where the character seems to be struggling with this dragon—places where this big emotional conflict becomes visible. Let me show you one such moment." I opened the book (to page 190). "I'm going to show you a specific moment in the story that supports your thinking."

"It's in that last chapter we read together, after Percy, Grover, and Annabeth have defeated Medusa. Grover asks Percy to explain more about their quest, about why they are seeking Zeus' lightning bolt. I copied parts of it for you. The first part begins with Percy asking Grover a question."

■ *Teachers, at this point I read aloud the part of the text that starts with Percy asking Grover: '"How are we going to get into the Underworld?" and read on until Grover says to Percy: "OK, Percy. Whatever." Basically, choose about one page of text that clearly shows that characters have problems outside of those that are explicitly part of their quest. You'll notice that I oriented the readers to this moment in the story by recalling it and retelling what led up to it. You may want to give your readers a copy of the page you choose, as I do here.*

"Readers, this moment seems packed with evidence for your theories about these characters' dragons, doesn't it? Take a moment to analyze it, and then go back into your conversation, but this time, really use some specifics from the text to support your theories."

They did.

Link

Inspire your readers to think about the dragons in their own lives, as well as the lives of their characters.

"Readers, this was a lot. Today you learned to think metaphorically about the dragons that characters face. You learned to zoom in on moments in the text, where these dragons become visible. You learned some Latin: *Hic Sunt Dracones.* Let's go off to read, friends, and I'll be looking across your notes and your conversations to see where you are noticing, that *Hic Sunt Dracones*! I'll also be curious to hear about your investigations into the dragons in your lives. After all, one reason we read is to have more insight into our own storylines."

What's This Story Really About?

Thinking About Themes and Life Lessons

Getting Ready

▶ Read through the end of Chapter Fourteen in *The Lightning Thief*, or to a part of your read-aloud novel where it is clear that the character is learning important lessons and that the reader can, too.

▶ Have *The Paper Bag Princess* on hand.

▶ Call to mind the fantasy novels you are reading. I use *Lord of the Rings* because this tale of the young hobbit is commonly known through film and print—it is part of cultural literacy. Frodo, like Wilbur in *Charlotte's Web*, has become a classic character.

Connection

Tell a story about a fellow reader who speaks of books in terms of their themes and life lessons, not their plots or characters alone.

I tell about how I spoke with an avid reader of *Lord of the Rings*: "'Jackson,' I said, 'why do you keep rereading this story? After all, you know what happens with the hobbits and the elves and so forth. What makes this story so important to you?'"

"Jackson stared at me. I thought at first that I had hurt his feelings, that he wasn't going to answer. But he was just building up steam. When he did speak, the words came out in a torrent. 'Mary,' he said, 'this story isn't about hobbits and elves. This story is about the struggle between good and evil. This story is about how power slowly eats away and corrupts. This story is about how the physically strong can use their gifts to protect others. This story is about how even the smallest and physically weakest can find moral strength to defeat evil. This story is about love and how love drives us to be better than we are.' Jackson stared at me again. 'That's why I keep reading this story,' he finally added. 'It's teaching me how to live. And I'm not an elf.'"

"'Oh,' I said. 'Well then. I think I'll get back to these elves and hobbits. Clearly I have a lot to learn from them.'"

"Friends, you can imagine that this was a humbling moment for me. Here I had been, following Frodo across Middle Earth, adoring Aragon and Legolas, laughing at Gimli the dwarf, detesting Gollum. I had been deeply involved in these characters and the problems they faced. But it seemed as if I was missing what these stories were really about. Frankly, readers, I realized that the story was so exciting that I was basically a plot junky!"

Name your teaching point. Specifically, teach your students that stories are not just about what happens, they are also about underlying themes and life lessons.

"Readers, today I want to teach you that often with great stories, the plot is a vehicle for teaching about ideas. The stories are not just about what happens. Stories are also about themes and life lessons. Insightful readers mine these stories for these themes and lessons."

Teaching

Recall some familiar fantasy tales and retell them in terms of themes and lessons. Then demonstrate on the read-aloud text how to mine the story for possible themes.

"Readers, fantasy novels are incredibly helpful in teaching us how to mine literature for themes and lessons. That's because fantasy is almost always about a struggle between good and evil: that's the most common—indeed, essentially universal— theme of fantasy stories. In the plot, there are usually clearly delineated characters who represent good and others who represent evil. As you witness these characters struggle—even though you are not an elf—you can learn about this theme. Think about *Star Wars*: on the one side, Darth Vader and the forces of darkness, on the other, young Luke Skywalker and his valiant Jedi companions. Friends, you don't have to *be* a Jedi knight to learn from Luke about how hard it is to struggle against evil, how you struggle to be strong, how hard it is to trust yourself, how you have to learn from your mistakes, and go on."

▓ *Teachers, I use* Star Wars *because I assume that, like* Harry Potter, *it has entered into cultural literacy. These stories demonstrate a literary tradition, the way that* The Hunger Games *is part of a dystopian tradition that emerged most strongly with Orwell. Use whatever characters and narratives you think your readers will be familiar with. Sometimes I show a very short film clip (one to two minutes) as a demonstration text.*

"One way that readers do this work is by asking ourselves at any time in our reading: what is this story beginning to be about?" And then, as we recall the story, instead of focusing on the plot, we try to mine the story for big themes and life lessons. It's actually not that hard to do; it's just really easy to *not* do, if you're a plot junky like I am. Watch me do this work, with *The Lightning Thief*. So, instead of saying that this story is about satyrs and demigods, I'm going to push myself to say: so far, what is this story beginning to be about?"

I picked up the book, and looked at all our charts and timelines. "Well . . . so far, Percy has been struggling to figure out his powers. In fact, he's rather like Luke Skywalker. He doesn't really know how strong he can be yet, and so he's always testing himself, a little further each time. Let me see, what evidence do I have for that? Well, in the part we just read, where Percy dives off the St. Louis arch to save that little child from the Chimera, Percy definitely goes further than he's ever gone before. He really puts his own life on the line. So, if I ask myself about the life lessons that Percy is learning, I guess he's learning that he can be a better person than he ever thought possible. And he's learning that inside of himself, he has special powers. Now, if that's what Percy *learns*, what does he teach? Let's see, sometimes in these moments, characters teach each other lessons. Well, I guess Percy taught this boy that sometimes strong people defend weaker people. Hmm . . . that's interesting to me. I've always been preoccupied with the problem of bullies and how to stand up to them. Wow! I could even think of the Chimera not as a literal monster but, metaphorically, as a bully! And Percy shows how to stand between bullies and their prey."

I looked up from the book, which I had been holding open to this page. Then I continued. "But what about *me?* What if I move to what lessons Percy teaches me? I'm not a demigod. But I guess I'd like to believe that inside all of us is the ability to be strong. I don't want to leap off the St. Louis arch, but I'd like to be able to stand between bullies and those they pick on. And I'd like to become stronger, as I grow, than I was as a child. Not physically stronger but more sure of myself, more willing to get into the fray."

I looked up. "Wait, this is working! Now that I'm thinking hard about this theme—that all it takes to stand up to bullies is courage—I'm even realizing that it's not Percy's demigod powers that make him so incredible during that battle on the arch. It's his compassion and his courage that make him incredible. And those are qualities that any of us can learn more about. Aha! I'm starting to be onto something."

■ *It's helpful for kids if you set your 'reading realizations' off with some drama, so that you emphasize these moments of epiphanies. Their passion for reading work is fueled by yours. Also, you want to make it easy for them to 'see' what work you are doing.*

"Readers, do you see how I thought back over the story, thinking first about what's been happening in the story, and then asking myself what the story could really be *about*? And when I did this work, friends, I didn't try to make some cliché, grand statement, the kind that might be on a bumper sticker (or a state exam: main idea). Instead, I tried to find lots of words for what I was thinking, and I went back to the story to find some moments that made this theme, or lesson, visible. Also, readers, if you're stuck, follow the same process I did: think about what lessons characters learn, and then move to what they teach each other. That may bring you to lessons they teach us."

Active Involvement

Give your readers a chance to practice this work, preferably on an accessible text.

"Readers, even simple fantasy stories often have powerful themes."

I held up *The Paper Bag Princess*. "Why don't you try this work now, using *The Paper Bag Princess*? If that feels successful, move on and try mining the story you are reading for themes and life lessons. Ask yourself: what is this story beginning to be about? And remember, stories can be about more than one theme, and they may teach more than one lesson. So, keep saying to yourself: what else could this be about?"

■ *Teachers, I modeled on* The Lightning Thief *and gave students a chance to try this work on* The Paper Bag Princess *because the latter is a more accessible text and its themes are more readily apparent.*

"Friends, as I listen to your conversations, remember to support your ideas by saying what in the story makes you think this. Sometimes, we have a tendency to start spouting grand themes or popular sayings, like 'don't judge a book by its cover.' But it's better to play around with your own language, and then return to moments in the story that seem to support your ideas. So go back to your conversations, but this time, try to say to each other: what in the story makes you say that?"

They did.

"Readers, another way to think about the themes and lessons in the stories we read is to consider which ones matter the most to us personally. When I think about *The Lightning Thief*, for instance, there are so many important themes and life lessons: that it's hard to lose people we love; that it takes a long time to really discover who we want to be; that inside us, sometimes, are special powers; that our friends can stand by us; that we can recover from big mistakes. But not all these themes matter equally to me, right now in my life. So, I may consider the many possible meanings of a story and decide to focus on one or two that seem significant to my own learning. For instance, I am interested in the idea that we can recover from big mistakes. Clearly Grover has gone on since his bad incident on his first quest. He has continued to seek half-bloods and to try to protect them. He hasn't lost faith in himself. That is really important to me. I tend to be haunted by my mistakes. I relive them in my thoughts. I wish I could go back and change things. But this book is teaching me that it's also important to move on. Do you see how I took a personal angle on the themes and lessons, thinking about which meaning might be important to me? You can do this, too, in your conversations or in the writing you do in your notebook."

Link

Send your readers off, reminding them to consider what their stories may really be about.

Remind your students that the story has to unfold a bit, before they start saying to themselves, "What is this story starting to be about?" Also, stories are about more than one thing, so keep reminding readers to develop multiple ideas.

■ *As young readers begin to explore theme, they'll tend to slip into cliché (such as, "It's about how all that glitters is not gold") or decide on one theme and ignore other possibilities or parts of the story that don't fit. So we have to keep celebrating that complex stories are about more than one idea and that complex readers have more than one idea about their stories.*

There's No Such Thing as True Good or Evil

Characters Are Not Usually All One Way

Getting Ready

▶ Finish *The Lightning Thief* or your read-aloud text.

Connection

Tell a story about a reader who describes that characters are never fully evil or fully good, or talk about a friend or a character on a television program, such as Sue in Glee, who is more than one way.

"Friends, recently I was talking with a couple of young friends. One is a sixth grader, Jackson, who adores the *Harry Potter* series. We were talking about Professor Snape and about how awful he is to Harry. For a teacher, he really is incredibly cruel. He taunts Harry, he misjudges him, and he punishes him, sometimes unfairly. I was saying how much I detested Snape—he's everything I *don't* want to be as a teacher! But Jackson, who also dislikes Snape, nevertheless reminded me that Snape was not all bad. 'Listen,' Jackson said, 'characters are not all bad or all evil—there's no such thing as true good or evil.' Then he reminded me of how Snape sometimes protects Harry, and how Snape tries to serve Dumbledore. It's true, I thought. Characters aren't all one way. They may be good but still be flawed, and it's hard to sort out the character flaws from the evil character. Snape is a perfect example of that. It won't be until the final chapters of Book Seven of *Harry Potter: The Deathly Hallows*, after the reader has journeyed through almost four thousand pages of the story, that we find out whose side Snape has been on all along."

Name your teaching point. Specifically, teach your students that characters are complicated: they are usually more than one way. Experienced readers are alert for the character flaws in the hero and the admirable traits in the villains.

"Readers, today I want to teach you that as the books we read become more complex, the characters also become more complicated. They are not just all evil or all good—they are nuanced. This means that powerful readers delve deeply into their characters' strengths, flaws, and motivations across the whole arc of the story."

Teaching

Analyze a character from the read-aloud text, looking for signs that he or she is more than one way.

"As the characters in your stories become more complicated, friends, you have to do more complex reading work. You can no longer simply list character traits. Characters shift. They are unpredictable. They may be good but have significant character flaws that get in the way of them being good all the time. I'm thinking, for instance, of Poseidon, in *The Lightning Thief.* At first, he seems cruel and selfish. He has, after all, abandoned Percy. He left Percy's mother. Here's what Percy says about Poseidon":

> I felt angry at my father. Maybe it was stupid, but I resented him for going on that ocean voyage, for not having the guts to marry my mom. He'd left us, and now we were stuck with Smelly Gabe. (39)

"And Poseidon can be rather childish. Annabeth, daughter of Athena, says:"

> One time my mom caught Poseidon with his girlfriend in Athena's temple, which is *hugely* disrespectful. Another time, Athena and Poseidon competed to be the patron god for the city of Athens. Your dad created some stupid salt-water spring for his gift. (157)

"So, Poseidon didn't protect Percy from monsters. He didn't even claim Percy as his son. But then, with each

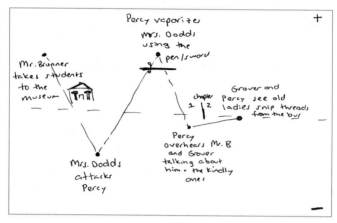

FIG. 7.1 *Emotional timeline of events*

encounter with Poseidon, we find out more about him. I found out that Poseidon rules a big kingdom, and he seems a little overwhelmed with the problems of this underwater kingdom. I found out that he worries about justice and if Zeus will do what is right. Finally, I see that Poseidon can be funny and affectionate. In fact he shows Percy several times that he loves him. I even began to feel sorry for Poseidon, to wonder what it must be like to have children who will not live as long as you do. I realized that Poseidon wasn't bad, he was just complicated."

■ *Teachers, if you want to add to their writing-about-reading practices, this is where you could show your kids an emotional timeline you've made, of Percy's relationship with Poseidon (see Figure 7.1). When making such a timeline, I jot a dotted line for the neutral state of a character's emotions, or the relationship. Then I put moments above the timeline that are positive, and moments below that are negative, with rising and falling related to the intensity of the emotion. You end up with a kind of EEG, an emotional timeline that depicts our analysis of character' emotions.*

Active Involvement

Set up your students to try analyzing a character. Remind them of a character from the read-aloud text who is complicated.

"Readers, do you see how I thought about a character, and how I thought about that character across the whole book? And I tried to consider all the incidents this character is involved in. I thought hard about the character's strengths and flaws, about behaviors and motivation, and I tried to be sympathetic. I also expected that the character would be nuanced, would be more than one way."

"Readers, stories you are reading are full of characters who are like this: good characters who have significant character flaws, characters who are bad but who, in some ways, you admire, and even characters who deceive us! *The Lightning Thief* is full of characters like this, who are complicated. Perhaps the most complex and surprising character is Luke, who we consider a hero at the beginning of the story and who shows himself to be a villain at the end."

"Let's give you a chance to try this work. Open up your notebooks to see what you've been jotting about characters as you've been reading. Recall any specific incidents where you saw that they were flawed, or admirable, or complicated. You may want to flip through your book to find some specific moment. You could also think about *The Lightning Thief* if you want to practice this work now. You could choose to practice by delving into Luke's character, in which case, really push yourself to remember what you know about Luke and why he behaves the way he does. I'm going to give you a few quiet moments to think."

I did. They looked in their notebooks and books. Then, after a few minutes had passed, they began to turn and talk. After another few minutes, I gathered them back.

Link

Send your students off to read, first reflecting that characters in our lives, like characters in our stories, are often complicated.

Archetypes, Quest Structures, and Thematic Patterns

You could break this lesson into three lessons: one on archetypes, one on quest structures, and one on themes. I make that decision based on the expertise of my readers and on the pressures of time—I may teach them all and then go back to each lesson separately afterward, or I may introduce them and simply hope that some readers will be intrigued enough to keep going.

Connection

Tell a story about a reader who predicted a major plotline because of his or her knowledge of story structure and archetypes.

"Friends, I want to take you back in time to a few years ago, just before Book Six of the *Harry Potter* series—*Harry Potter and the Half-Blood Prince*—was released. Well, friends, in the months just before the book was released, there was a lot of press about it. Someone from the publisher had leaked that a major character would die in the novel. Fans everywhere met and tried to surmise who it would be. Would it be Ron, Harry's volatile best friend? Would it be Hagrid, the loyal gamekeeper at Hogwarts? Would it be malevolent Professor Snape, who detests Harry?"

"I vividly remember sitting with my friend Torrin, who is an expert on all things *Harry Potter* and a prolific fantasy reader. Torrin was only in middle school at the time, but he was certain that it would be Dumbledore who would die. 'It has to be Dumbledore,' Torrin explained calmly to me. 'Dumbledore has to die because he's the mentor, and the mentor has to die so the hero can come of age.' I was flabbergasted. Torrin was so certain. And, as the whole world knows, he was right."

"I realized, as I spoke with Torrin, that he was having a richer experience reading these books because he had certain expectations about them. Torrin read each story in the shadow of all the other fantasy stories he knew, and he was constantly, almost unconsciously, comparing and evaluating them."

Name your teaching point. Specifically, teach your students that an understanding of story structure, character roles, and themes deepens readers' analysis and extends readers' literary conversations.

"Friends, today I want to teach you that fantasy novels have certain characteristics or patterns in their structures and the character roles. One way that experienced fantasy readers analyze the stories they read, therefore, is to consider the patterns that emerge in story structure, character roles, and themes—these are part of the literary traditions of this genre."

Teaching

Explain about quest structures, archetypes, and universal themes more fully, and demonstrate how you use these lenses to analyze part of the read-aloud text.

"Let me show you how this works, readers. I'm eager to share this knowledge with you because when Torrin explained to me some of what he knew about fantasy, I found the experience of reading these novels to be even richer. I found that I better understood some of the roles of the minor characters. I began to ask myself, for instance, when a character was introduced: what role might this character play in the story? I began to realize that obstacles placed in the hero's path were also moments of moral choice. I worried about character flaws in the hero because I came to *expect* that a character flaw could have tragic implications for others. In fact, it probably would, which means there was increased tension in the story. Knowing more about the patterns in fantasy literature illuminated the nuances of these stories, built even more tension for me as a reader, and, ultimately, gave me even more satisfaction. It's really satisfying to feel that you are becoming more expert in something."

"Readers, fantasy experts often evaluate their stories within certain predictable aspects: story structure, character role, and theme. Most fantasy novels follow a quest narrative structure: the hero is given a quest, which means he or she must journey to achieve something. Sometimes the quest involves rescuing a captive or sacred object, as with *Shrek* or *Sinbad*. Other times the quest may ask the hero to destroy a villain or a dangerous object, as with *The Lord of the Rings* and the *Harry Potter* books. And the other common quest narrative is that the hero has gotten into another world or place and the quest is the journey out of there, as with *Alice in Wonderland* or *The Hunger Games*."

■ *Here's where, teachers, you might decide to continue this lesson, about quest structure, as one lesson on its own. I'm condensing here, and going on to add other predictable aspects of this literary tradition.*

"Another predictable aspect of fantasy novels is that the characters often play expected roles in the story. The main character is usually the hero of the story. But common hero-types include the *traditional* hero, such as Prince Caspian; the *reluctant* or everyday hero; the ordinary person who finds himself or herself swept into great events, such as Harry Potter or Katniss; and the *anti-hero*, who usually has non-heroic traits. He may cheat, lie, steal, or be cruel, yet he or she plays a heroic part in the drama. Other common character roles in fantasy include the mentor, who teaches and guides the young hero; the companions, who usually accompany the hero on the quest; and the villain, who is often disguised and can even appear to some to be benevolent, like the Queen in *Narnia*. And there is often a consort, who is the love interest of the hero, if the story is one that has a romantic aspect. Readers, what's interesting about these character roles is that each of these characters will be important to the story and that they'll often have many similarities across fantasy stories. It's common for one of the companions to be jealous and volatile, for instance. It's common for the mentor to perish before the hero comes of age. It's common for the villain to have many guises. It's common for the hero to be uncertain of his or her powers. In this way, the characters in fantasy stories are not just their individual selves, they are also *archetypes*, which is what we call standard characters. It's an added dimension to these characters, and it can be an added dimension to your reading work."

■ *Again, you might make this a separate lesson at this point. I often show some film clips, to bring up vivid examples of these kinds of characters.*

"Finally, the third common aspect of fantasy stories is that they are almost always about the epic struggle between good and evil, and in fantasy, by the end, good triumphs. In this way, fantasy stories are moral triumphs. They demonstrate that the struggle against injustice is worth it, no matter how arduous the journey is. A common theme in these fantasy novels, though, is that the character has to overcome internal struggles and embrace his or her essential goodness in order for good to triumph for all. Self-sacrifice is one of the most important themes in fantasy. The hero can't sulk in his tent like Achilles at Troy. The hero must put himself or herself in danger's way. That's one reason these stories are so inspiring. They propagate a code of chivalry and honor."

"Now watch as I evaluate a fantasy story for these traits. I think what's interesting is to compare stories we're reading to these traditions. So I'm going to compare *The Paper Bag Princess* and *The Lightning Thief*. Watch how I use my knowledge of these common aspects of fantasy to compare the narrative structure, archetypes, or themes of these stories."

I held up both books. "Well, let me try analyzing the narrative structure. Let me think about how each of these structures compares to a quest structure. *The Paper Bag Princess* . . . well, Elizabeth certainly follows the dragon in order to get Ronald. She does make this journey, and on the journey she overcomes several obstacles set by the dragon. And in *The Lightning Thief*, Percy also goes on a quest. In fact, Chapter Nine is called, 'I am Offered a Quest!' But now let me *really* compare their quests. Elizabeth makes her own quest; no one tells her to follow the dragon, whereas Percy is given his quest. And Elizabeth *understands* her quest: she knows what she is searching for and what's in the way, whereas Percy's quest is set by the gods, and he doesn't really understand all of it. Also, Percy has companions on his quest; Elizabeth has to do it all alone. Let me see, what else . . . well, each character changes on the quest. They both come to some pretty huge realizations. In the final moments of their quests, Elizabeth rejects Ronald, and Percy accepts his father. I guess that's bringing me into character analysis, so now I could talk more about them as archetypes. That would be an interesting way to compare them."

Active Involvement

Rally your readers to use these lenses to analyze and compare the stories they are reading.

"Readers, do you see how I compared one predictable aspect of these stories, thinking about how fantasy usually goes, and then using that as a lens to think across the stories? I used the lens of the quest narrative structure as one way to compare these stories. And do you see how sometimes we start out with similarities, and then we evaluate the differences as well in these narratives? It's in these nuances that fascinating new ideas are hiding. Why don't you give that a try with your club—try comparing the story structure in your novels to *The Paper Bag Princess* and *The Lightning Thief*. You might ask yourself: how are the quests the same or different? What kinds of obstacles tend to appear during the quest? How much do characters change, and what happens in the quest to cause these changes? When they fulfill the quest, what happens then? Give it a try—it's an interesting way to compare stories and extend your conversations."

They did. After a bit, I pulled them back.

"Readers, so far, we've been comparing the quest structure. I heard your conversations and they were very intriguing. Some of you looked closely at the obstacles, and you were saying that there seem to be a few different *kinds* of obstacles that are put in the hero's path, including physical tests, mental tests, and moral tests. The *Deltora Quest* series readers, in particular, were explaining all the different obstacles that Lief faces in the first book and showing how each obstacle was a sort of test. I think that's a fascinating way to think about it. It makes me think more about *The Paper Bag Princess*, for instance, because if I think about her encounter with the dragon as a test of her strength, her intellect, or her character, it does give me new things to think about. Elizabeth decides not to use her strength. That's clear. So she uses her intellect and tricks the dragon. On the other hand, she wins through manipulation, flattery, and trickery, which means maybe she still had some growth to do as a character. *That* makes me think that maybe her last obstacle is a character test—and it's Ronald, not the dragon! Wow, friends, this is all really cool. I also heard some of you saying that some of Percy's obstacles may be inside him, that he needs to learn to trust his friends, and his father. That means, a few of you said, that there's more to think about as some of us move into the second book in the series. I heard you say that maybe Percy's quest isn't over by a long shot, that maybe this first triumph is just one obstacle. That's really insightful friends. And it's just *interesting*, right? There is a way in which comparing these aspects of fantasy leads to really interesting conversations."

■ *You'll notice that at each stage of this minilesson, I'm restating what we've said and what the readers do, to coach them in this intellectual, expert, and highly analytical reading work. Clearly, if you broke this lesson into three lessons, you'd substitute an active engagement for each sub-category, rather than have multiple active engagements, as we have here.*

"Let's try the archetypes. Consider any of these stories and their characters: Elizabeth, Percy, Wiglaf, Harry, their companions, their mentors, the villains. . . . Let's see what happens when you compare the roles these characters play in the stories you are reading. Or maybe you prefer to talk about themes and compare what these stories seem to be about."

They talked. After a bit, I called them back.

"More fascinating conversation, readers! I heard some of you comparing Percy to Harry. You were noting how they both seem like reluctant heroes: they start out unsure of their powers. They are young, not yet of age. They each grew up as an ordinary boy. Then each is thrown into something epic. Hidden in each seem to be special strengths. And I heard you comparing the moment when Percy fights the Chimera with the moment when Harry fights the basilisk. You said that each boy, under stress, becomes extraordinarily valiant, even though in ordinary moments both boys can be flawed. Hmm . . . more to think about. And I heard others of you compare Wiglaf from the *Dragon Slayers' Academy* series to Elizabeth. She doesn't seem to feel any guilt about tricking the dragon, you said, but Wiglaf is grief-stricken that he killed a dragon. In fact, he finds that his quest makes him unhappy, which none of us really knew what to think about until someone said that maybe this, too, is just Wiglaf's first obstacle; it's not really the end of his quest."

Link

Celebrate this intellectual work, and send them off as readers ready to carry literary traditions in mind as they read. They can add that lens to their reading work and analyze their novels with added expertise.

"Readers, as you go off to read today, you'll be a different reader, because you'll know that the book you are holding doesn't exist all alone; it's part of a grander tradition. You might use your notebook to do some reflecting on how you see some of your characters fulfilling archetypal roles. You might chart how your characters play some of the same roles as these *kinds* of characters in other books. You might chart your character's quest on a map or timeline. For our gallery walk this Friday, let's see if we can bring some artifacts that demonstrate how we're doing this thinking. It's a different way to read, to think that the decisions an author makes might be influenced by the literary traditions of the novel; that the characters exist not just in their own relationships but in relationship to characters in other novels; that the themes you are discovering in one novel may run through several of your novels as a literary tradition. Then you'll have intellectual work in discovering the nuances of how they're different as well. It's sort of amazing—it makes your book and you part of something bigger. I am eager to see the results of your thinking."

Reading Across Texts with Critical Lenses

Representation, Stereotypes, and Gender Norms

Getting Ready

▶ Have on hand some book covers and possibly some film clips or images you've downloaded of Disney characters. I print from a few pictures of the Little Mermaid, Cinderella, and so forth from the Internet.

▶ Many fantasy series have blogs and websites for their readers. You may let students do some quick online research to see what images are posted to accompany their texts, what characters may look like in the film versions, and what other readers are saying about these interpretations.

Connection

Describe characters you like in the read-aloud, and compare them to other favorite characters.

"Friends, gather around. I've been rethinking my favorite parts of *The Lightning Thief.* I find myself thinking about favorite characters, and what I like and don't like so much about them. Sometimes, these character traits seem to be related to traits I've seen in other characters. It's a little bit like what we discussed yesterday, about archetypes. But it seems a little different as well—it's about stereotypes, too. I'm just pondering how the characters in the novel fit with my expectations of young male and female characters."

■ *Teachers, for this lesson, I often have available, from the Web, some images of current supermodels, of Disney heroines, and of characters from movies and novels. You could include Hermione from the* Harry Potter *series and Bella from* Twilight. *You'll notice that, universally, they are slim, graceful, with clear features, and usually have long hair. They are Annabeth. Do the same for the male heroes and you'll see a parallel representation emerge. In Disney, you can be brave, as long as you are beautiful. If a character has a physical disability in a fairytale, for instance, that damage is meant to symbolize a damaged soul. That kind of repeated aligning of difference with something damaged is something we want to interrupt with critical literacy lenses. Beauty does not actually mean that someone is good or brave.*

Name your teaching point. Specifically, teach your students that one way readers analyze stories is with critical lenses, being alert to stereotypes and gender norms.

"Readers, today I want to teach you that one way readers analyze a story is to read with critical lenses for representation, stereotypes, and gender norms (or rules). One way to do this work is to consider characters' actions and appearances."

Teaching

Demonstrate analyzing a character in terms of how he or she fits stereotypes and gender norms or demonstrates a certain representation.

"This is really fascinating work, readers. Let me show you a little bit about how it goes. First, one way you can analyze a character is to compare that character to others by his or her appearance. I just showed you how I thought about the Disney characters, for instance, and realized that all those female characters reinforce a stereotype that girls have to look like Barbie dolls in order to be important. A stereotype is a typical way of thinking about things: that girls have to be beautiful or that boys have to be strong, for instance. Stereotypes can be really damaging, because they make individuals feel as if they don't fit. Some stereotypes are negative, and that's not fair. So I'm happy that Annabeth doesn't fit the stereotype of 'beautiful blonde' with her looks. I'm not completely happy—she *is* blonde. It does say often that she is beautiful. It would have been cool to have a girl who maybe wasn't so stereotypical in her looks. And I'm also concerned about issues of representation. I'm not seeing characters of color in many of our fantasy novels, and I'm rarely finding gay characters. So another way to characterize Annabeth is that she fulfills a hetero-normative (typically straight), white representation. That's not all she is—she's more than those things, but she's also those things, and I might analyze how she fulfills some of those roles."

"Another way readers analyze a character is by his or her actions. Readers ask themselves: does this character act in ways that are unusual? In particular, you can look for how a character reinforces or breaks with gender norms. Gender norms are the rules associated with being a girl or a boy—those invisible rules that aren't written down but that we all seem to know. One of my favorite stories is *Oliver Button Is a Sissy*, and it's about this boy who wants to tap dance, but his father and his classmates all think that boys shouldn't dance; boys should play football! In fact, before we go any further, think for a moment about an idea you have, or used to have, about what boys and girls are allowed to do, and then share with your partner."

They did.

"Friends, I heard you say things like boys aren't allowed to wear dresses. Others said that girls are supposed to be polite and to take care of people. Some of you said that girls aren't supposed to fight. A lot of you said that boys learn not to play with dolls. Friends, there is nothing inevitable about any of those rules. We learn them from the books we read, the films and television we watch, and the people who surround us. One thing I like about Annabeth is that she breaks with a traditional gender norm that girls should be polite and pretty. She is really strong, and she fights! In fact, I think she fights better than Percy! So she fits some traditional female roles, and she transgresses some. She dates boys, and she is graceful, slim, beautiful, and blonde. And she uses weapons, fights monsters, and is a strategist. She's a complicated mix."

Active Involvement

Give your students a chance to practice this work, reminding them of some characters and stories that might get them started.

"Readers, do you see how I thought about what characters look like and what they do, what they are and what they aren't, to think about how they break with or conform with stereotypes and gender norms, and how they fulfill certain representations and leave others unfulfilled in the novel? Let's give you a chance to try this work. You could keep going with *The Lightning Thief*, or you could turn to the characters in the stories you are reading. I know that the readers of the *Deltora Quest* books will be eager to talk about Jasmine and Lief and how they mix up traditional girl-boy roles. And what about Eric/Erica in the *Dragon Slayers' Academy* books? Isn't she the best 'knight' in their school? I want to listen to that conversation!"

"I often find it helpful to compare characters, to talk about more than one, when I do this work. Give it a try, really thinking hard about how the characters' appearances and actions fit with or break with stereotypical roles and norms."

■ *Teachers, you could decide to extend this teaching by also showing how characters fit into certain norms of relationships and sexual identities. Are there any gay characters in the stories? Do all the girls and boys end up dating, or are other possibilities shown? Do nontraditional family structures get honored? You could also look at characters' fates—who gets to survive?*

Link

Tell your readers that they can read critically whenever they encounter text as well as television and film. Send them off to read, with an extra alertness to how characters with disabilities, characters of diverse ethnicity and culture, characters who make personal choices about sexual identity and love, and characters who are transgressive are represented.

Bringing Our Expertise in This Literary Tradition to Our Reading Plans

What's Next for Ourselves as Readers?

Getting Ready

▶ Have on hand some fantasy series, some historical fiction, or some complex fiction of any genre.

▶ Prepare your charts from the unit to list the strategies you've been teaching.

Connection

Recall the work your readers have been doing, in a celebratory tone.

■ *Teachers, when we start and end a unit, we have oppor-*
tunities to help students learn to reflect and to self-initiate,
developing the habit of asking themselves: what's next for
them as readers? How will they outgrow themselves? What
reading work will they pursue? How will they incorporate
and extend their current studies? You may want to give
them the opportunity to revise and annotate their notebooks
and to rearrange the charts in the room, keeping up and
revising only what seems needed. They often can incorporate
the charts into a few new ones.

Name your teaching point. Specifically, teach your students
that readers make opportunities to reflect on their work
and make plans for how to incorporate and extend it.

"When readers have been deeply studying a genre, we may
incorporate and extend this work. Some ways to do this include: using the strategies we have sharpened in other genres; seeking more books, and company, to become even more
expert in this genre; or moving to other genres that are similar to this one."

Teaching

Instruct the readers to use their notes to reflect on their
reading work and demonstrate how a reader might make
plans for future work at this point.

"Readers, there is no one way to think about this. But it seems
to me that some of the strategies you have been practicing,

such as writing as you read, thinking about story structures and archetypes, delving into themes and life lessons, and considering stereotypes and gender norms, might be interesting work in your independent reading. We have some charts here, and you have your notebooks as well. Readers use these tools to remind themselves of what they have learned. Their notebook is almost like a manual for future work."

"It's also possible that some of you want to go on. Readers do become more powerful by becoming deeply passionate and expert in a genre. They read series, they move up levels, they keep reading and writing and talking, and they become deeply passionate about certain series, and probably about certain authors. If you want to become that kind of fantasy reader, you'll need to become an active seeker of books, and you'll want to build your own social groups around reading. I imagine you'll be looking in the library and bookstores, and trading among your friends, for all the great fantasy series that are out there. You'll become experts in authors; you'll know when the next book is coming out; you'll be a passionate, informed reader. If this is how you want to extend our work, you may want to make some lists of future reading and possible book clubs you could launch. Powerful readers take charge of their reading lives and follow their passions to the fullest."

"Readers, there's one more way that you might want to extend this work that I'd like to teach you about today. When you become expert in a genre you adore, you can also think about what other genres are related to, or similar to, this one, as a next step for you as a reader. And friends, historical fiction might be a logical next step for some of you. Like fantasy, historical fiction happens in other places and times. Like in fantasy, there are exciting events and intense characters. Like fantasy, historical fiction tackles the struggle between good and evil. The stories suggest powerful, disturbing, and inspirational themes and lessons. Historical fiction can be hard. It's harder to find series, or lots of books by an author, so you have to be someone who learns to find books if you want to read a lot of historical fiction. But I truly think that a lot of you would love it, and that you'll find stories to love."

Active Involvement

Give your readers an opportunity to reflect and plan.

"So, readers, do you see how I'm suggesting that you make a plan for your reading life? As you make this plan, consider how to use the strategies you've been learning in fantasy, in which case you'll want to turn to your notebooks and our charts to remind you of those; or how to go on in fantasy, seeking books, finding reading partners, and becoming even more passionate and expert; or turning to another genre, such as historical fiction, which offers up many of the rewards and challenges you encountered so beautifully in fantasy."

"Turn and talk, and then I think you should open up your notebook to a fresh page and do some writing. Really reflect on how fantasy reading has made you a more powerful reader. Describe your plans for your reading life. It's so important to take these moments, to allow ourselves to harness what we've learned and make some decisions for what's next."

They talked, then I suggested they should do some writing.

They wrote.

Link

Celebrate, and send them off!

"Friends, this has been an epic journey. I'm proud of your work. I'm eager to see what you'll do next. I'd be honored to be in some of your fantasy or historical fiction book clubs, if you start some. Off you go."

Some of the Greatest Fantasy Series That Get Kids Hooked on Reading

The Werewolf Club	(L)	Daniel Pinkwater
Unicorn's Secret	(M)	Kathleen Duey
Secrets of Droon	(M-O)	Tony Abbott
Spiderwick Chronicles	(Q-R)	Holly Black and Tony DiTerlizzi
Dragon Slayers' Academy	(N-P)	Kate McMullan
Time Warp Trio	(P)	Jon Scieszka
The Edge Chronicles	(R-U)	Paul Stewart and Chris Riddell
Deltora Quest	(R-T)	Emily Rodda
Warriors	(R-S)	Erin Hunter
The Chronicles of Narnia	(T)	C. S. Lewis
Rowan of Rin	(T)	Emily Rodda
Animorphs	(T-U)	K. A. Applegate
The Ranger's Apprentice	(T-U)	John Flanagan
Underland Chronicles	(U-V)	Suzanne Collins
A Series of Unfortunate Events	(U-V)	Lemony Snicket
Artemis Fowl	(W)	Eoin Colfer
Percy Jackson and the Olympians	(U-W)	Rick Riordan
Dark Is Rising	(X)	Susan Cooper
Redwall	(Y-Z)	Brian Jacques
Time Quartet	(X-Y)	Madeleine L'Engle
Harry Potter	(V-Z)	J. K. Rowling
The Mortal Instrument Series	(Y-Z)	Casandra Clare
The Golden Compass	(Y-Z)	Philip Pullman
Dragons of Pern	(Adult)	Anne McCaffrey
Lord of the Rings	(Adult)	J. R. R. Tolkien

continues on next page

Manga—Fantasy Graphic Novels		
Pokemon	(P-Q)	
Naruto	(R-S-T)	
Yu-Gi-Oh	(T-U)	
Dystopian Literature		
City of Ember series	(R-U)	Jeanne DuPrau
Maze Runners Trilogy	(V-W)	James Dashner
The Hunger Games series	(X-Y)	Suzanne Collins
The Giver series	(Y-Z)	Lois Lowry
Fahrenheit 451	(Y-Z)	Ray Bradbury
Forest of Hands and Teeth series	(X-Y)	Carrie Ryan
The *Incarceron* series	(Y-Z)	Catherine Fisher
Brave New World	adult	Aldous Huxley
1984	adult	George Orwell

*A note on these reading levels. Reading levels vary according to which source you access, which site you visit, to which expert you talk. These levels—which are, like all upper levels, subjective (based on vocabulary, length, structure, and content)—are influenced not only by the Fountas and Pinnell guided levels but also by the experience of colleagues and teen readers, who can become remarkably astute at recognizing what makes one novel more complex than another.

ACKNOWLEDGMENTS

This small book sits on the shoulders of some grand readers, most specifically, Jackson Ehrenworth, Torrin Hallett, Tanner Hallett, and Dylan Parker Nagel. Tanner recommends fantasy series, Jackson devours them, Torrin provides a discerning judgment, and Dylan finds links to online sites and the cornucopia of manga delights. They are truly voracious and powerful readers, who, along with the kids I see reading and talking in schools, in subway trains, on buses, and on planes, give a vision of how enticing fantasy novels are, and how complex these readers are.

Any collection of reading lessons builds on the work of Lucy Calkins and all my colleagues at the Reading and Writing Project, including those who are still there, and those who were there before me. In this case, the tone of these lessons, in how they hope to elevate the independent reading practices of teen readers, is most heavily indebted to Donna Santman, not only to her brilliant book, *Shades of Meaning: Teaching Reading and Comprehension in Middle School*, but also to the times when I have been lucky enough to be in a classroom as she teaches or coaches. Donna consistently demonstrates how hard teens want to work and will work, if they are surrounded by high expectations and clear instruction and structure. Another key influence is Colleen Cruz, who has been teaching about fantasy for years now.

She has been a spokesperson for its importance, and most importantly to this work, she consistently, generously and openly, shares book lists, reading strategies, and her deep knowledge of the traditions of this literature. Colleen is a mentor to me in intellectual generosity. Finally, Garrett Kyle is the adult I know who is always first to know about new YA fantasy novels, to read them, and to insist that we read them too—to our delight.

Thank you especially to Teva Blair, for her discerning editorial skills, and her judgment. She knows just when to be concise and when to elaborate. I learned a lot from Teva as a writer on this project.

Finally, there are two people who continue to provide glorious writing and teaching opportunities to me, as well as opportunities to hone my practice, debate ideas, and develop shared passions and thinking. Lucy Calkins of the Reading and Writing Project, and Kate Montgomery of Heinemann, thank you! You invited me to write this book, and it was, as always, such a pleasure to write, think, and work with you.